Manhattan Panorama

Manhattan

Photographs by Aldo Sessa

Panorama

RIZZOLI
NEW YORK

For Lisl Steiner

First published in the United States of America in 1992 by
Rizzoli International Publications
300 Park Avenue South, New York, NY 10010

Library of Congress Cataloging-in-Publication Data

Sessa, Aldo, 1939–
    Manhattan panorama / photographs by Aldo Sessa
        p.   cm.
    ISBN 0-8478-1589-7
    1. Manhattan (New York, N.Y.)—Pictorial works.
    2. New York (N.Y.)—Pictorial works. I. Title
F128.37.S47   1992
779'.997471—dc20
                        92-9226
                        CIP

Page 1: View of towers surrounding St. Patrick's Cathedral from East 50th Street.

Frontispiece: View from Fifth Avenue and West 24th Street of towers surrounding Madison Square.

Photographs by Aldo Sessa

Designed by Pamela Fogg

Printed in Singapore

Preface

It was love at first sight. Our relationship began back in 1962 when, while crossing the Brooklyn Bridge, an attractive silhouette rose before my eyes. Since then I find myself compelled to return to her as often as I can. Each trip is an attempt to rekindle my passionate desire to unearth her secrets.

Manhattan must be one of the world's most photographed places. Just as hundreds of writers have written of its charms, so have millions of amateur and professional photographers snapped the same shots over and over again. In my attempts to distinguish this portrait of the city from those of my colleagues and predecessors, it occurred to me that I might achieve a more personal effect by working with the panoramic camera. In that way I could cover a wide visual field, recording scenes of the city with the same breadth of vision that the glance of the human eye can. I feel that this camera permits the surroundings to enhance what would be the central focus of an image captured by more conventional means.

Manhattan is a one-of-a-kind phenomenon, where the mixture of architectural styles, singular sounds, mind-boggling rhythms, and truly tall buildings—turning people into insignificant specks—blend before the senses in an intriguing union. In discovering every corner of the city I found myself obsessed with capturing every angle as well. However, I tried to conceal my mission as photographer, carrying just one camera so that I might go unnoticed. If I happen to be at the right place at the right moment, I can shoot without interference or preconceptions. I cloaked my camera in black tape, transforming it into a dark, difficult-to-identify object, loaded my backpack with film, and took to the streets. I found myself alone in a snow-covered Central Park and among masses of bodies being swept into the subway at rush hour. These contrasts, like so many others, turned the Manhattan I was witnessing through the viewfinder into a mesmerizing kaleidoscope of shapes and patterns. Being of the conviction that laziness is the photographer's worst enemy, I scaled every staircase I came across, seemingly buried myself in the snow that carpeted city parks, slipped on ice in a most ungracious fashion, moved like a feline across bridge girders, had a few unsavory encounters on the West Side, and, as a finale, forgot my camera in the back seat of a taxicab.

This book is a tribute to a city that granted me access to some of her secrets. Even after so many years of posing so patiently for me, I still love her with the same intensity I felt on our first meeting.

Aldo Sessa

Overleaf: Lower Manhattan from the Hudson River

Statue of Liberty

Brooklyn Bridge

South Street Seaport

Overleaf: World Trade Center Towers

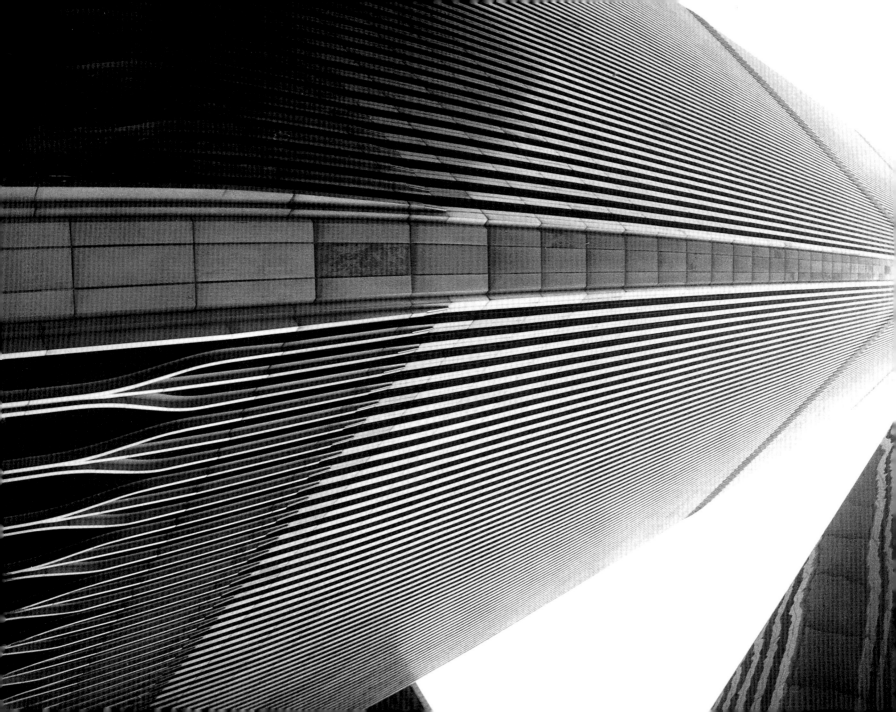

Wall Street from the porch of the Federal Hall National Memorial

Looking north up Broadway from Bowling Green, Financial District

Overleaf: View north from World Trade Center Observation Deck

Concourse, World Trade Center

Escalators, World Trade Center Concourse

Plaza, World Trade Center

Taxi Stand, Avenue of the Americas at Watts Street

Vegetable Stand, Canal Street, Chinatown

Fish Market, Canal Street, Chinatown

Thompson Street, Soho

Broome Street, Soho

Parking Lot, Prince Street, Soho

Prince Street, Soho

Overleaf: Balducci's, Avenue of the Americas at 9th Street, Greenwich Village

Second overleaf: Jefferson Market Library, Avenue of the Americas at 10th Street, Greenwich Village

Sculpture Yard, East Village

Overleaf: Mural, Tribeca

Shadows, Fifth Avenue

Union Square

Overleaf: Washington Mews, Greenwich Village

Second overleaf: Gramercy Park

Flower and Plant District, Avenue of the Americas at West 28th Street

Annex Flea Market, Avenue of the Americas at West 26th Street

View of Metropolitan Life Insurance Company Tower from East
24th Street and Park Avenue South

Overleaf: Flatiron Building, Fifth Avenue at 23rd Street

Main Post Office, Eighth Avenue at West 33rd Street

Lobby, Empire State Building

Empire State Building, Fifth Avenue at 34th Street

Overleaf: View north from the Empire State Building Observatory

View north at night from Empire State Building

View south at night from Empire State Building

View to the northeast from Empire State Building

Overleaf: The Chrysler Building, reflected in glass sheathing of the Grand Hyatt Hotel, Lexington Avenue at East 42nd Street

Pan Am Building, Grand Central Terminal, Grand Hyatt Hotel,
Chrysler Building from East 42nd Street and Vanderbilt Avenue

Overleaf: Main Concourse, Grand Central Terminal

Reading Room, New York Public Library,
Fifth Avenue at 41st Street

New York Public Library, Fifth Avenue at 41st Street

Citicorp Center, Lexington Avenue at East 53rd Street, evening

Overleaf: View of Citicorp Center and "Lipstick" building from
Third Avenue and East 53rd Street

Paley Park, East 53rd Street between Madison and Fifth Avenues

Fountains, Time-Life Building, Avenue of the Americas at West 50th Street

Overleaf: Mid-block plaza, West 46th Street near Avenue of the Americas

Second overleaf: The Waldorf-Astoria Hotel, Park Avenue at East 50th Street

Shop window, Cartier, Fifth Avenue at 52nd Street

Jewelry Vendors, Fifth Avenue at 57th Street

Atrium, Trump Tower, Fifth Avenue at 56th Street

Overleaf: Queensboro Bridge

F.D.R. Drive near East 53rd Street

Overleaf: View of United Nations Building and towers along the
East River from Roosevelt Island

Walkway below Beekman Place

West 57th Street at Avenue of the Americas

Overleaf: General Electric Building, Lexington Avenue
at East 51st Street, evening

Stretch Limousine, Park Avenue

Times Square

Times Square

Port Authority Bus Terminal, Eighth Avenue at West 41st Street

Lunch Carts, West 50th Street and Avenue of the Americas

Overleaf: Marquee, Radio City Music Hall, Rockefeller Center,
Avenue of the Americas at West 50th Street

West 44th Street between Broadway and Eighth Avenue,
the Theater District

Overleaf: Rear façade, Roseland Ballroom, West 53rd Street
between Broadway and Eighth Avenue

57th Street and Seventh Avenue

51st Street Subway Station, Lexington Avenue IRT

View of Central Park West apartment buildings from Central Park

Overleaf: Polar Bear, Central Park Zoo

Second Overleaf: Tavern-on-the-Green, Central Park West at West 67th Street

Central Park

Central Park

Central Park

Overleaf: Wollman Skating Rink, Central Park

Lincoln Center, Broadway at West 65th Street

Overleaf: View east from Central Park South, including Hotel Pierre,
Sherry-Netherland Hotel, and General Motors Building

View to the northeast from GE Building, Rockefeller Center

Rockefeller Center Plaza, Winter Skating Rink

Rockefeller Center Plaza, summer

The Plaza, Fifth Avenue at 59th Street

The '21' Club, West 52nd Street off Fifth Avenue

Overleaf: View west from Third Avenue and East 58th Street

INCREDIBL

ALEXANI

IBM Building Atrium, Madison Avenue at East 56th Street

Waterlilies by Claude Monet, The Museum of Modern Art,
West 53rd Street off Fifth Avenue

Ancient Art Gallery, The Metropolitan Museum of Art,
Fifth Avenue at 82nd Street

Entranceway, Whitney Museum of American Art,
Madison Avenue at East 75th Street

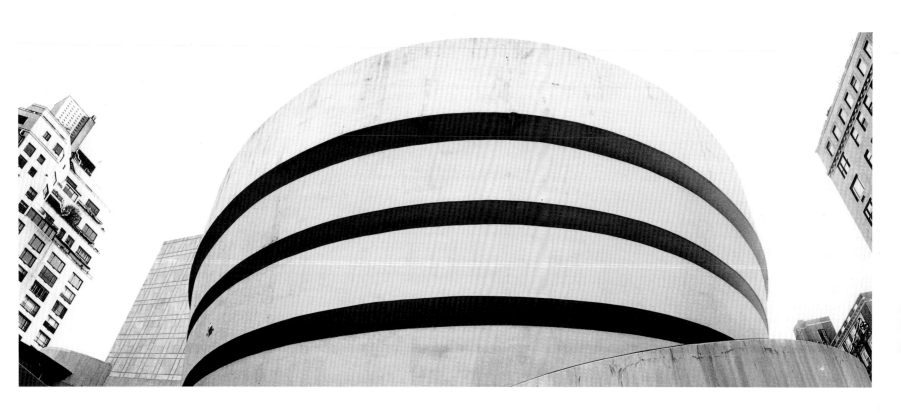

The Guggenheim Museum, Fifth Avenue at East 89th Street

Overleaf: Interior, Guggenheim Museum, with artwork by Jenny Holzer

Second overleaf: Cooper-Hewitt Museum, Fifth Avenue at East 91st Street

Gracie Mansion, East End Avenue at East 88th Street

The Frick Collection, Fifth Avenue at East 70th Street

Columbia University

Parking lot and mural, Harlem

Overleaf: Soldiers' and Sailors' Monument, Riverside Park,
Riverside Drive at West 89th Street

George Washington Bridge, Hudson River at West 187th Street

The Cloisters, Fort Tryon Park

Henry Hudson Bridge, Harlem River, Upper Manhattan

Acknowledgments

Alberto Caputo

Aldo Sessa

Gianfranco Monacelli, Robert Janjigian, and Pamela Fogg, Rizzoli International Publications

Lisl Steiner, Luis Sessa, Alberto Caputo, for their assistance

Lexington Labs, New York, for development and processing

Daniel Nuñez, for printing

Teresita Sessa

Valeria Sessa Saguier

Encarnacion Ezcurra

Edward Shaw

Philip Grushkin